THE KINGDOM'S GOSPEL

Themes In Sharing The Good News of the Kingdom

Jhun Ma

Copyright © 2024 Jhun Ma

All rights reserved

The characters and events portrayed in this book are fictitious. Any similarity to real persons, living or dead, is coincidental and not intended by the author.

No part of this book may be reproduced, or stored in a retrieval system, or transmitted in any form or by any means, electronic, mechanical, photocopying, recording, or otherwise, without express written permission of the publisher.

ISBN-13 : 979-8321319741

Cover design by: Canva.com

*With boundless love and heartfelt inspiration,
I dedicate this book to my lovely wife, Babes, who
joyfully fills my life.*

*To our incredible children, Jed, Jacob, and John,
who bring endless joy. blessings and meaning to
our journey.*

*To the Tuao Church of Christ and Pasir Panjang
Church of Christ your unwavering support and
encouragement motivate me to serve the Lord
passionately.*

*May our Heavenly Father's glory shine through
every page as we honor our King Jesus and
embrace the guidance of the Holy Spirit.*

43But he said to them, "I must proclaim the good news of the kingdom of God to the other cities also, for I was sent for this purpose."

JESUS, LUKE 4:43

CONTENTS

Title Page
Copyright
Dedication
Epigraph
Preface
Part One — 1
STARTING OUR JOURNEY — 2
LIVING OUT THE GOOD NEWS — 5
IT'S OUR TURN TO SHARE — 9
Part Two — 12
The Bible: Its Purpose and Importance — 13
Sin: the Bad news — 17
The Kingdom's Gospel: — 21
Israel: A Kingdom Of Priests & A Holy Nation — 25
The Ten Commandments: — 29
The Kings and Kingdoms: — 33
Exile and Restoration: — 37

Jesus Christ	40
Repent and Believe:	44
Confession and Baptism:	49
On Baptism:	53
Part Three	58
On Being A Disciple:	59
The Church:	64
Our offering	68
New Heavens and New Earth:	72
Conclusion	77
Afterword	81
Pledging Our Allegiance:	83
Acknowledgement	87
About The Author	89
Praise For Author	91

PREFACE

"The Kingdom's Gospel: Themes in Sharing the Good News" takes you on a journey to explore the true meaning of the Gospel. It represents the culmination of my spiritual growth and understanding as I tried to grasp the amazing importance of God's powerful acts of saving us. I studied the Bible, learned from theological ideas, and gained knowledge from respected ministers, preachers, and church members to write this book.

The purpose of "The Kingdom's Gospel" is to help you understand the Gospel's saving power, as shown in the sacred texts. It goes beyond a shallow understanding of the Good News and invites you to deeply explore God's Kingdom and how it affects every aspect of our lives.

In these pages, I want to show you that the Gospel is not just a set of beliefs or rules to follow. It is a vibrant message, a compelling call, and a way of life. An incredible encounter with Jesus Christ, the Lord, and King can change your life forever. "The Kingdom's Gospel" reveals the unique plan of God to redeem us, His authority and rule, and the endless hope it offers to all people.

As you join me on this journey, I hope that "The Kingdom's Gospel" will inspire you to go deeper into understanding God's Kingdom, embrace the life-changing power of the Gospel in your own life, and join the mission of sharing this Good News with others so they can also become followers of Jesus Christ.

May these words inspire, challenge, and guide you as you explore the depths of the Kingdom's Gospel and discover its eternal relevance for today's world. May you experience the tremendous grace, boundless love, and mighty power of King Jesus, transforming your life through the beauty of the Gospel.

With sincere gratitude and excitement,

"Jhun Ma"

PART ONE

*This part of the book prepares us for the need
to know the Gospel themes and its content.*

*"Starting Our Journey" sets us on an exhilarating
path of faith in how we live as disciples.*

*"Living Out the Good News" calls us to embody
the Gospel's transformative power.*

*"Our Turn to Share" is an inspiring story
about a musician and his friends
and the lesson of their story empowers us
to the joy of being a part of the mission
given by our Lord and King, Jesus Christ*

STARTING OUR JOURNEY

38 Peter said to them, "Repent and be baptized every one of you in the name of Jesus Christ so that your sins may be forgiven, and you will receive the gift of the Holy Spirit.

- **Acts 2:38**

Now that you have accepted the Lord, repented of your sins, and decided to follow Him as your Lord and King through water baptism, a great challenge lies ahead. You may find yourself wondering, "What's next?"

In this moment of heartfelt appreciation, we embark on a journey of worshiping God the Father through His Son, Jesus Christ, guided by the overflowing presence of the Holy Spirit. We look to the early disciples as our examples, those who formed the foundation of the renewed Israel, the People of God.

In Acts 2:41-42, we witness the birth of the early church. Those who embraced the message of Jesus were baptized, and on that day alone, about three thousand individuals were added to their number. They dedicated themselves to the apostles' teaching, fellowship, the breaking of bread, and prayers.

Preachers and ministers encourage us to live a life of loving God and loving others as we gather for worship. Deep in our hearts, we feel compelled to share the incredible salvation and eternal love God has graciously bestowed upon us. We naturally share our faith, recounting stories, testimonies, and new experiences since encountering Jesus. However, we recognize that there is something more required in our sharing.

We desire for our listeners to appreciate our stories and be persuaded to follow Jesus, just as we have. We long for them to experience the same salvation and life-changing transformation that we have witnessed. We want them to accept Jesus into their lives, to be saved, and to embark on a journey of discipleship.

In our quest to share the Good News, we yearn for

a natural, easier, and more sensible approach that resonates with those we encounter and leads them to a genuine decision to follow Jesus. This book aims to reveal how our church community shares this life-transforming message that has saved us and changed us to be more like Jesus.

Within these pages, you will discover the key themes in sharing the Kingdom's Gospel so listeners will submit to and embrace the Kingship and Lordship of Jesus in their lives. Together, we will uncover these key themes to effectively communicate the Good News and invite others to embark on a life-altering journey with Jesus.

Are you ready to dive into the challenge of sharing the Gospel in a natural, accessible, and compelling manner? Let us embark on this great adventure, knowing that as we faithfully carry the Great Message within us, lives will be touched, hearts will be transformed, and the kingdom of God will expand.

Prayer:

Blessed are You, O Lord, King of the Universe. Thank you for the salvation that we have in Christ Jesus. Help us share this message of new life with others. Amen.

LIVING OUT THE GOOD NEWS

2 You yourselves are our letter, written on our hearts, known and read by all, 3 and you show that you are a letter of Christ, prepared by us, written not with ink but with the Spirit of the living God, not on tablets of stone but on tablets that are human hearts.- **2 Corinthians 3:2-**

Before we can share the Good News with others, they must first see the good news in us. As bearers of the Kingdom's Gospel, we must manifest God's reign in our lives. Each day presents an opportunity for us to live a life of worship, just as the apostle Paul encouraged the believers in Rome.

Paul exhorts us in Romans 12:1; We should offer our bodies as living sacrifices that are holy and pleasing to God. This is a reasonable act of worship for us. Worship is offering our lives by living like Jesus, reflecting His life through our own.

"To begin each day, let us cultivate the habit of prayer. Open your day by praying to the Father and speaking to Him heart-to-heart. Remember that God listens to you as His beloved child. When you find yourself unsure of what to pray for, take comfort in the prayer Jesus taught His disciples, known as the Lord's Prayer (Matthew 6:9–13):

As your faith grows, the Spirit will lead you to utter your own prayers. When we don't know how to pray, the Spirit intercedes for us, aligning our prayers with God's desire through the yearnings of our hearts (Romans 8:26–27).

Allow the Holy Spirit to guide you in all aspects of your life. Give the Lord your goals, dreams, and ambitions. Allow the Holy Spirit to permeate your thoughts, influencing your judgments, actions, and everything you say and do. Remember to express gratitude to the Father in the name of the Lord Jesus in all your endeavors. (Colossians 3:17).

Reading the Bible is another important spiritual exercise. Make a particular time to study God's Word. Reading God's Word allows Him to communicate with us in the same way that prayer will enable us to commune with Him. It links us to God's people throughout salvation history and invites us to join in the story of redemption, sanctification, and the mission to make disciples of Jesus (Psalms 1, 119; Matthew 28:18-20).

By practicing the discipline of reading and meditation on His Word, the Lord will shape our minds, thoughts, and actions to be more like Jesus. This practice fills us with the Holy Spirit's presence and guidance, providing us with true freedom and transformation that will lift our spiritual heights of glory, resulting in even more glory for the Lord (2 Corinthians 5:15–18).

The fellowship and encouragement of other believers are vital on your Christian life journey. Every first day of the week, gather with your brothers and sisters in faith to praise the Father through the Lord Jesus, by the power of the Spirit. Edify and encourage one another, bearing the fruits of the Spirit and witnessing personal progress (Hebrews 10:23-25; Galatians 5:22-23).

With these spiritual practices, you become a visible message to the world as you live out the Good News. Others will be drawn to our Lord's love and grace as a result of your transformed life and the oneness of the body of Christ. May your life be a testament to the power of the Gospel of the Kingdom, influencing people around you and bringing glory to God.

Prayer:

Blessed are You, O Lord, King of the Universe. Thank you for this new life you have given us. Empower us to live a life like Your Son, Jesus, so others can see the good news in us before we share the good news of Your Kingdom.

IT'S OUR TURN TO SHARE

And he said to them, "Go into all the world and proclaim the good news to the whole creation.- **Mark 16:16**

A prominent Italian composer named Giacomo Puccini graced the stage in the enthralling world of music. His amazing operas attracted audiences all around the world, garnering him recognition and adoration from music lovers everywhere.

However, there was a dark cloud that hung over Puccini's life. He was fond of smoking Toscano cigars and cigarettes, which would finally lead to his death. Puccini was diagnosed with throat cancer, a serious condition. He had radiation treatment to tackle this heinous disease. Unfortunately, the treatment caused uncontrollable bleeding, and on November 29, 1924, Puccini's heart couldn't take it anymore, and he died of a heart attack.

Outstanding operas like "Madame Butterfly" and "La Boheme" marked Puccini's illustrious career. Nonetheless, his final work, "Turandot," remained unfinished at the time of his death.

When Puccini died, his opera remained unfinished, awaiting the finishing notes. But by God's grace, music masters have stepped forward to carry on his legacy. With the help of Puccini's drafts, his friend and composer Franco Alfano completed the final two scenes of "Turandot." The great conductor Arturo Toscanini, a personal friend of Puccini, assisted Alfano in this quest.

Finally, one year and five months after Puccini's death, on April 25, 1926, the full version of "Turandot" took its first breath. The grand premiere occurred at La Scala in Milan, and Arturo Toscanini directed the orchestra. Toscanini did something extraordinary as the concert neared the end of Puccini's work. He hesitated before turning to face the crowd and saying, *"This is where the master ends."* The air was filled with a profound quiet. Toscanini added, raising his baton once more, *"And this is where his friends began."* The opera resumed as a monument to friends' and disciples' devotion and affection for their dead leader.

Dear friends, we have arrived at a similar point in the Gospels. We have arrived at the point in time when Jesus, the Master, completes his earthly work. The story, however, does not finish here. Just as Puccini's friends and disciples continued his work, Jesus' disciples and friends kept on his mission.

We will explore the main themes of their message, the Kingdom's Gospel, which draws inspiration from the Hebrew and New Testament scriptures, the Lord's ministry, and the Great Commission He gave to His apostles. Let us remember that we are not alone as we explore the teachings and experiences of Jesus and his disciples. We stand on the shoulders of those who came before us, echoing their faith and carrying the gospel flame into the world.

Prayer:

Blessed are you, Lord God, King of the Universe, for granting us the bearer of this good news of the Kingdom. Empower us to share this joyful message with others as our expression of love for You and Your Son, Jesus Christ. Amen!

PART TWO

This part unravels the Kingdom's Gospel and its core concepts. The Old and New Testaments precisely describe God's magnificent work of salvation. As we progress, we discover the amazing Good News that the prophets, Jesus, the apostles, and the early disciples preached. The Gospel is not a sequence of steps to salvation, spiritual laws, or marks of the true church. The Gospel proclaims the Kingdom of God's Arrival through Jesus' death, burial, resurrection, and anointing as Lord and Savior.

THE BIBLE: ITS PURPOSE AND IMPORTANCE

"The Bible is the ultimate source of wisdom and guidance for all of humanity." - **Abraham Lincoln**

The word "Bible" has its roots in the Koine Greek and Latin phrase "ta biblia" (τὰ βιβλία), which means "the books." Its singular form, "biblion" (τὰ βιβλία), refers to a "scroll" or "papyrus roll," reflecting the early form of books. Over time, the term "Bible" has come to represent a collection of sacred texts that are considered authoritative in Jewish and Christian religious traditions.

The Bible is categorized into two primary sections: the Old Testament and the New Testament. The Old Testament, written in Hebrew and Aramaic, is also known as the Hebrew Scriptures or "TANAK" (an acronym for *"Torah," "Nevim,"* and *"Ketubim"* which means the Law, the Prophets, and the Writings). It consists of the foundational books from Genesis to Malachi (in Jewish order, the 2nd Chronicles is the last book) and contains the Jewish scriptures that bear witness to the history and prophetic revelations of the Israelite nation.

The New Testament, primarily written in Greek, focuses on the life, teachings, death, and resurrection of Jesus Christ. It begins with the four Gospels, which provide accounts of Jesus' ministry and teachings, followed by the Book of Acts, which records the birth and growth of the early Church. The remaining books consist of Epistles or Letters written by apostles and early Christian writers, offering guidance and encouragement to believers. The final book, Revelation, provides an apocalyptic glimpse into the lives of early Christians and the future judgment of God.

The Bible serves a primary purpose, as Apostle Paul emphasized to Timothy, his evangelist trainee. In 2 Timothy 3:15, Paul reminded Timothy that the sacred scriptures instruct and lead people to salvation through faith in Jesus Christ. Paul's reference to *'sacred writings'* pertained to the Hebrew Scriptures, which were already compiled and translated into Greek, known as the Septuagint version (*LXX*).

The scriptures are described in 2 Timothy 3:16–17 as "inspired" or "God-breathed" (*"theopneustos"*), indicating that the very breath of God or the Holy Spirit guided the writers. As such, the scriptures are valuable for teaching, rebuking those who do wrong, correcting misguided paths, and training individuals in righteousness. Through continuous study and practice, believers can grow, mature, and fulfill their God-given purposes.

Acts 17:11 reveals the proper approach to studying the Bible. It highlights the receptiveness and eagerness of the Berean Jews, who examined the scriptures daily to confirm the truth of the message presented to them. This practice embodies the three "E's" of scripture study: being Eager to accept, Examining diligently rather than merely listening, and engaging in Everyday study. Neglecting these three aspects may lead to laziness and the missed opportunity to embrace the gift of salvation offered through the message of the sacred scriptures.

Those who read and heed the words of the scriptures are blessed. The scriptures not only guide believers toward eternal life but also invite them to experience a vibrant and intimate relationship with Jesus. By drawing near to Jesus, they can truly receive the blessings that come from embracing and applying the teachings found within the holy scriptures.

The Bible, comprised of numerous books written over centuries, holds a profound significance. Understanding its origins, structure, and purpose allows individuals to appreciate its message and its transformative power. By eagerly studying and examining the scriptures daily, one can grow in faith, find guidance, and experience the blessings of a vibrant relationship with God and Jesus in the presence of the Holy Spirit.

Prayer:

Blessed are you, Lord God, King of the Universe, who gave us Your Word for our salvation through the Holy Scriptures. Help us eagerly examine it every day of our lives. Amen.

SIN: THE BAD NEWS

"The problem of sin is not merely a moral issue; it is a spiritual and existential struggle within each of us."

*- **Henri Nouwen***

This world is facing a problem that goes beyond the conflicts we see in various parts of the world. It's a problem that everyone can feel—a sense that something is missing, that something is not quite right. As we explore and learn more, we come across mysteries that are hard to explain. One of these mysteries is what we call sin—a concept that leaves us puzzled. In both the Hebrew and Greek Scriptures, sin is portrayed as a problem that affects all human beings. It reminds us that we all fall short of the high standards set by God (Romans 3:23). In this chapter, we will delve into the Hebrew term *"chata'ah"* and the Greek phrase *"hamartia,"* which will help us understand the profound impact of sin on humanity.

Let's start by looking at sin in the Hebrew Bible. The term *"chata'ah"* means *"missing the mark"* or "straying from the path God intended." In the stories we find in the Hebrew Scriptures, this word represents sin and shows us how easy it is for anyone to go astray from the path of righteousness. Take, for example, the story of Adam and Eve. They made a choice that went against God's plan and had serious consequences. The Hebrew Scriptures also give us guidelines and regulations that reveal the destructive effects of sin. They emphasize the importance of repentance, forgiveness, and reconciliation. They teach us to take responsibility for our sins and seek ways to restore our relationship with God.

In the Greek New Testament, sin is described as "hamartia," which means "a departure from God's standards leading to separation from God" (Isaiah 59:1-4). It signifies falling short of what God expects from us or failing to reach the glory He intended for us (Romans 3:23). The writers of the New Testament stress the devastating consequences of sin and emphasize the need for salvation through Jesus Christ (Romans 6:23).

So, what has sin done to humanity? Throughout history, sin has caused destruction, pain, and broken relationships with God, with others, and with ourselves. Sin leads to the mistreatment of the vulnerable and a disregard for the value of human life. It damages our reputation and prevents us from reaching our full potential, trapping us in a cycle of self-hatred.

The effects of sin echo through generations, causing ongoing conflict and division. Corruption, violence, and oppression thrive when sin dominates a society. Prejudices and biases flourish in the presence of sin. Even the natural world suffers because of how humanity mistreats God's creation (Romans 1:18–32; 8:20–22).

But there is hope, even in the midst of this seemingly hopeless situation. The Kingdom's Gospel, which is the good news of Jesus Christ, brings hope for redemption, reconciliation, and restoration. These themes appear throughout both the Hebrew and Greek Scriptures. God's grace has the power to transform individuals and heal broken relationships. With God's help, we can overcome the consequences of sin and work towards a world where righteousness, justice, and peace prevail for all.

Understanding the impact of sin on humanity requires us to consider both the Hebrew and Greek perspectives. Sin ruptures our relationship with God, distorts our identity, and perpetuates despair and decay in the world. However, the entire story of the Bible reveals God's plan to bring us back to Him, offering us union with Him and forgiveness of our sins. In the upcoming chapters, we will delve deeper into these themes of union and forgiveness.

Prayer:

Blessed are You, Oh Lord, King of the universe, who loves us eternally in spite of our sins and wickedness. By your Fatherly Love You call us to return to Your Loving Embrace. In Christ Jesus, Amen!

THE KINGDOM'S GOSPEL:

The Good News of the Kingdom

"The gospel is the royal announcement that the crucified and risen Jesus, who died for our sins and rose again according to the Scriptures, has been enthroned as the true Lord of the world." - **N.T. Wright**

The word "gospel" holds a special place in Christian teachings. It comes from the Old English word "Godspell," which is a translation of the Greek word "euangelion." When we break down this Greek term, we find that "eu" means "good" and "angelion" means "news" or "message." So, the word gospel signifies the proclamation of good news or a joyful message.

In the sacred scriptures, the gospel is presented as the grand announcement of God's Kingdom through the redeeming work of Jesus Christ. It represents Jesus, who was crucified and rose from the dead, as the Scriptures foretold. He offered Himself as a sacrifice for our sins and was revealed to be the anointed King of Israel and Lord of the world. This good news lies at the core of the Christian faith.

The gospel holds great significance in the Hebrew scriptures because, as Isaiah prophesied, it brings salvation, joy, and peace. Isaiah 52:7 tells us, *"How beautiful upon the mountains are the feet of him who brings good news, who publishes peace, who brings good news of happiness, who publishes salvation, who says to Zion, 'Your God reigns.'"* This message of God's reign brings His people joy, comfort, and redemption.

Even before the exile of Israel, God had revealed His plan to establish an eternal kingdom through the lineage of David. In 2 Samuel 7:12–13, God made a promise to David that his descendant would become a king and establish a kingdom. This king would build a house in God's name, and his kingdom would endure forever. The prophet Daniel also received a vision of a mighty King who would be given authority, glory, and dominion. People of all nations and languages would serve this King, and His rule would never end.

These prophetic visions reveal God's plan for a future

King and the establishment of His eternal kingdom. They point to the Gospel, which proclaims the Reign of God through His Messiah, Jesus Christ. The Gospel brings hope, fulfills God's promises, and establishes an everlasting kingdom.

Understanding and embracing the Gospel as the Good News of God's Kingdom is crucial for our salvation and living in alignment with God's purpose. Through Jesus, the anointed King, we find joy, peace, and eternal life. Romans 1:16 highlights the significance of the Gospel, where the Apostle Paul declares that he is not ashamed of it. He affirms that the Gospel has the power of God to bring salvation to all who have faith, whether they are Jewish or Greek.

In Galatians 1:6-9, the apostle Paul passionately warns believers about the importance of staying true to the genuine gospel. He expresses astonishment at how quickly they have turned away from the true message of Christ and embraced false teachings.

Paul emphasizes that there is only one true gospel and warns against falling for false teachings or misinterpretations. He even goes so far as to say that if anyone, including himself or even an angel, preaches a different gospel, they should be considered cursed.

Let us rejoice in the Good News of God's Kingdom, knowing that through Jesus, our God reigns. May we actively share this message with others so they may experience the blessings, salvation, and eternal life found in the Gospel.

Prayer:

Blessed are You, O Lord, King of the Universe. We praise You for proclaiming the Good News of Your Kingdom as foretold by the Prophets and now revealed through Your Son, Jesus Christ, the Anointed Lord and King! Amen.

ISRAEL: A KINGDOM OF PRIESTS & A HOLY NATION

"Israel, both as a people and as a land, occupies a central place in the biblical narrative. It is a story of covenant, promise, exile, and hope. The very identity of Israel is intricately woven into the fabric of biblical history and theology." - **Walter Brueggemann**

Israel played a vital role in the proclamation of the Gospel, *which is the Good News of the Kingdom of God. As a visible political manifestation of this Kingdom, Israel was chosen and established by God, the Lord Yahweh. Through the three patriarchs—Abraham, Isaac, and Jacob—God's plan unfolded.*

Even in Abraham's time, the Gospel was being proclaimed. The apostle Paul confirms this in

Galatians 3:8, where he states that the Scripture foresaw God reckoning righteousness to the Gentiles through faith. The Gospel was declared to Abraham beforehand, with the promise that all nations would be blessed through him. Those who believe are blessed along with Abraham.

From the beginning, God intended to bless all nations through Abraham. In Genesis 18:18–19, God reveals His plan to Abraham. He promises to make him a great nation, to give them the Land of Canaan (Genesis 12), and he instructs him to teach his descendants to pursue righteousness and justice. Through their adherence to these values, all nations would experience blessings.

Israel began to take shape as a nation with the birth of Isaac and later Jacob, who became the patriarch of the twelve sons: Reuben, Simeon, Levi, Judah, Dan, Naphtali, Gad, Asher, Issachar, Zebulun, Joseph, and Benjamin. These 12 sons of Jacob became the ancestors of the Israelite tribes, each of which formed a distinct division within the nation of Israel. Before they fully became a nation, God made a covenant with them at Mount Sinai.

God had made a covenant with Abraham, promising blessings and establishing him as a mighty nation. He also made a covenant with the people of Israel.

Before giving them the Law, God declared, *"If you obey my voice If you stay true to my covenant, you will be highly valued and cherished among all nations. You will be a priestly kingdom and a holy nation"* (Exodus 19:5-6).

Through this covenant, the people of Israel became the first community of God, known as the Israel of God. They served as holy people and a kingdom of priests and received inspiration from the Spirit of the Lord.

The apostle Paul affirms Israel's significance in our Christian life, emphasizing that they possess adoption, *glory, covenants, the giving of the law, worship, and promises. The patriarchs belong to them, and through their lineage, Christ, who is God overall*, blessed forever, came into the world (Romans 9:5).

Israel's role as a kingdom of priests and a holy nation is a testament to its unique position in God's salvation history. They were chosen to carry the promises of God and ultimately played a vital part in the fulfillment of those promises through the coming of Jesus Christ, the Messiah.

Prayer:

Oh Lord, King of the Universe, we praise You for calling Abraham and giving him promises so that You can bless us through him. We praise You for choosing Israel as Your chosen nation. Through them, we have come to know You as the True and Loving God who reigns in our lives through Christ Jesus. Amen!

THE TEN COMMANDMENTS:

The Righteousness & Justice of God

"The Ten Commandments provide a moral framework that transcends cultures and generations, reminding us of our responsibility to love God and love our neighbors as ourselves." - **Max Lucado**

In the land of Israel, a special set of rules held great significance for the people. These rules were known as the Ten Commandments and served as the nation's constitution. They were not just ordinary rules; they encompassed two crucial aspects: righteousness and justice. These commandments were part of God's command for Abraham and his children, revealing their nature under God's rule and expressing His expectations for their relationships with Him and others.

Let us take a closer look at the content of these commandments, also known as the Law, Instructions, and Words, as written in Exodus 20:1–17. God had chosen the descendants of Abraham to be a nation, and He sealed this covenant by giving them the Ten Commandments. These commandments were like a special gift, showing the Israelites how to live in harmony with God and with one another.

The first part of the commandments focused on righteousness, which meant having the right relationship with God. The first four commandments were all about their connection with God. *Primarily,* they were commanded to have the Lord, whose name was YHWH, as their only God. This meant acknowledging His exclusive authority over their lives. *Secondly,* they were directed to worship the true and living God, turning away from idols and false gods. *Thirdly,* they were called to honor and revere God's name through their actions and words, showing respect for His holy name. *Lastly*, they were encouraged to set aside a day of rest, the Sabbath, to acknowledge God as their provider and to find rest in Him.

The second part of the commandments focused on justice, which meant having the right relationships with others. The remaining six commandments dealt with various aspects of fair and just interactions with fellow human beings. *The Fifth Commandment* instructed them to honor their parents, recognize the importance of family relationships, and treat their parents with respect. *The Sixth Commandment* urged them to value and protect life, promoting justice in their dealings with others. *The Seventh Commandment* emphasizes faithfulness in marriage, upholding justice within the sacred bond of matrimony. *The Eighth Commandment* reminded them to respect the belongings of others and to be honest in their dealings. *The Ninth Commandment* encouraged them to speak the truth, promoting justice through their words. Lastly, *the Tenth Commandment* warned against coveting what belonged to others, reminding them to be content and fair in their desires.

These Ten Commandments served as a comprehensive guide for the Israelites, covering their relationship with God and their relationships with one another. They laid the foundation for a righteous and just society, shaping the moral fabric of the nation of Israel.

By faithfully following these commandments, the Israelites developed a deep bond with God and created a society that reflected the Kingdom of God.

They showed their dedication to God's covenant by upholding righteousness and justice, embracing their role as God's chosen people, and embodying His principles in their daily lives. In doing so, they fulfilled the special purpose that God had given them as the children of Abraham.

Prayer:

"Blessed are You, Lord God, the Giver of the Commandments. Teaching us to live a life of righteousness and justice so we can be a blessing to the world."

THE KINGS AND KINGDOMS:

Agents of Righteousness and Justice

Kings may come and go, yet ultimate authority remains in the hands of the Lord, who reigns with unshakable justice, boundless wisdom, and unfailing love." - **unknown.**

During the era when the Law was given, there was a great prophet named Moses. *He served as the spokesperson of the Lord, leading the nation of Israel. After Moses, another leader named Joshua took over, guiding the twelve tribes to various parts of the Promised Land of Canaan. However, as time passed, the nation faced challenges in maintaining its faithfulness to the Lord.*

During a period known as the era of the Judges, the

tribes of Israel struggled to stay united and devoted to Yahweh. Their commitment to the Lord depended on the presence of a judge who would lead them. But whenever a judge died, they often turned away from God and began worshiping idols, becoming trapped in the cycle of sin.

Israel found it difficult to remain faithful to God during this time, as various appointed leaders governed them. Whenever these judges passed away, the Israelites frequently abandoned God and started worshiping idols.

In their sinful condition, they requested that a king rule over them, desiring to be like the nations surrounding them. This request angered the Lord because they had forgotten that He was their true King, reigning over them through the prophets and judges. It is written in Judges 21:25, *"In those days there was no king in Israel; everyone did what he thought was right in his own eyes."*

Despite their desire for an earthly monarch, God remained their ultimate king. In 1 Samuel 8:7, the Lord says to Samuel, *"Listen to all that the people are saying to you; they have rejected me as their king, and not you."*

The concept of the Kingdom of God was deeply intertwined with the nation of Israel. The anointed kings were entrusted with upholding divine order and promoting righteousness and justice among the people. Deuteronomy 17:18-20 emphasizes the importance of kings writing a copy of the law, reading it, and following its instructions.

However, throughout Israel's history, their kings often strayed from their divine mandate, leading the nation astray and causing great suffering. One such example is the story of King Solomon. As written in 1 Kings 11:4-6, *"For when Solomon was old, his wives turned away his heart after other gods, and his heart was not wholly true to the Lord his God."*

Due to Israel's persistent disobedience and idolatry, powerful nations conquered and captured them. Because of their actions, God allowed these nations to rule over Israel and drive them from their land. One of the most momentous events in their history was the Babylonian exile, also known as the Babylonian captivity. It lasted for about 70 years and left a profound impact on the Israelites. It began in 586 BCE when King Nebuchadnezzar II and the Babylonians conquered Jerusalem, resulting in the destruction of the Temple. As a stark reminder of the repercussions of failing to uphold righteousness and justice, this period of exile was characterized by great loss and suffering. The prophet Jeremiah eloquently lamented their actions, chronicling this tragic event in Jeremiah 32:30–35.

These examples highlight the importance of leadership that promotes righteousness and justice and the dangers of unfaithfulness and wickedness. They remind us that God alone is the true King, and His commandments are meant to be upheld. So let us learn from past mistakes and strive to walk in righteousness and justice, honoring God as our true King.

Prayer:

Blessed Are You O Lord, King of the Universe, who appointed Kings and established Kingdoms to manifest and realize the Righteousness and Justice You have planned for the whole world. Amen!

EXILE AND RESTORATION:

Judgment and Hope of Renewal

10 For thus says the Lord: Only when Babylon's seventy years are completed will I visit you, and I will fulfill to you my promise and bring you back to this place-
Jeremiah 29:10

Their sins marked the history of Israel and their disregard for the ways of the Lord. As a result, they faced punishment and exile. However, even amid their suffering, God did not abandon His people. He continued to speak through His prophets, offering them words of encouragement and hope. Let us delve into the prophecies and messages of hope and restoration revealed through the words of Jeremiah, Ezekiel, and Daniel.

The prophet Jeremiah was a bearer of hope for the exiled Israelites. He assured them that God had plans for their welfare and a future filled with hope (Jeremiah 29:11). Despite their captivity, God promised to listen to their prayers, restore their fortunes, and gather them from all the nations (Jeremiah 29:12-14). Jeremiah also foretold a new covenant that would renew Israel and Judah's relationship with the Lord (Jeremiah 31:31-34). This covenant would be different from the one broken in the past, as God would write His law on their hearts, allowing them to know Him intimately.

In his vision, the prophet Ezekiel witnessed the Spirit of the Lord departing from the east gate of the temple, symbolizing judgment and exile (Ezekiel 10:18-19). However, Ezekiel also received messages of restoration and hope. Through the vision of dry bones coming to life by the breath of prophecy, God demonstrated His power to revive His people and bring them back to life—a vision of resurrection (Ezekiel 37:1-14). This vision symbolized the restoration of Israel's spiritual vitality and their return to the Promised Land.

The prophet Daniel received visions that unveiled God's ultimate plan. In one of his visions, Daniel saw the Son of Man, a human figure, coming on the clouds of heaven and approaching God, who is known as the

Ancient of Days. God bestowed authority, dominion, and glory upon this Son of Man, signifying the establishment of a just and eternal kingdom (Daniel 7:13–14).

Through the voices of the prophets, God spoke words of hope and assurance to His people, even during their exile and sorrow. Jeremiah, Ezekiel, and Daniel's writings were just a few of the prophecies that conveyed God's steadfast love to Israel, His willingness to reestablish the covenant with His people, and the prospect of a bright future. These prophetic visions comforted and encouraged the Israelites in exile, reminding them that God was still mighty in His work in the world and faithfully advancing His divine plan for salvation.

Prayer:

Blessed are you, O Lord, King of the Universe. Despite Israel's sins and wickedness, You have shown mercy to them and revealed the depths of Your steadfast love for the world. Amen.

JESUS CHRIST

The Lord and King

"But these are written so that you may come to believe that Jesus is the Messiah, the Son of God, and through believing,]you may have life in his name." - ***John 20:31***

We journeyed with the nation of Israel through their struggles and their longing for a deliverer *who would rescue them from their failures and the oppression of other nations. They felt defeated, and their hope for a better future seemed to be slipping away. However, little did they know that God had a magnificent plan in store in His unwavering love and faithfulness to His covenant.*

God promised that all nations would be blessed through Abraham's lineage and his descendants. This promise reached its ultimate fulfillment in the person of Jesus Christ, who came to save His people from their sins (Matthew 1:1–21). Jesus is the embodiment of God's faithfulness to His promises.

The Scriptures had long foretold that the Messiah would come from the line of David. The Gospel of Matthew introduced Jesus not only as being from the lineage of Abraham but also as the Son of David, thus fulfilling this prophecy (Isaiah 9:6-7, Matthew 1:1). He is the long-awaited king who will establish an eternal kingdom marked by justice, righteousness, and everlasting peace.

Jesus boldly proclaimed the arrival of God's kingdom, declaring that it was already present among them (Luke 17:20–21). Through His miraculous healing and teachings, He demonstrated the power and authority of the kingdom. In Jesus, the Kingdom of God found its tangible and visible manifestation.

The Holy Spirit anointed Jesus, equipping Him to fulfill His mission (Luke 4:18–19; Acts 10:38). The Spirit dwelled within Him, enabling Him to bring good news to the poor, set captives free, and restore sight to the blind. Through Jesus, the Spirit's presence was no longer confined to the temple but became accessible to all through faith in Him.

Jesus redefined the law, emphasizing the paramount importance of loving God and loving others (Matthew 22:37–39). He taught that true obedience goes beyond mere adherence to outward regulations; it entails living a life of love and humble service to others. In the kingdom of God, the law finds fulfillment through love.

Out of His immense love for humanity, Jesus willingly sacrificed Himself on the cross. Through His death and resurrection, God granted forgiveness of sins and the gift of eternal life (John 3:16, Ephesians 1:7). His sacrifice brought redemption and restored the broken relationship between God and humanity. According to the prophet Ezekiel's prophecy, God anointed Him as the first fruit of the resurrection at His resurrection and proclaimed Him to be Lord and King (Acts 2:36).

All the accounts of Jesus' ministry point to His kingship. The Greek word for Christ is "Christos," which is a transliteration of the Hebrew word "Mashiach" or Messiah. It means "anointed one" or "chosen one" and refers to the expected deliverer and savior in Jewish tradition, who would fulfill various roles such as prophet, priest, and king. The term "Messiah" is used in both Hebrew and English to refer to the promised and anointed one in the Old Testament scriptures.

Jesus is the anointed Lord and King, fulfilling the promises of God and ushering in the Eternal Kingdom. This anointed one makes God's love, mercy, and salvation known to all. As we embrace Jesus as our Lord and King, we are invited to participate in His kingdom, living lives characterized by love, service, and forgiveness. In Christ Jesus the King, we find hope, redemption, and the fulfillment of God's ultimate plan for humanity.

Prayer:

Blessed are You, O Lord, King of the Universe. We praise You for anointing Jesus as our Lord and King, who saves and sanctifies us. Amen!

REPENT AND BELIEVE:

Allegiance to the King and His Kingdom

Repentance and faith are the twin acts of turning to Christ in the fullest sense. You can no more truly repent of sin without simultaneously trusting in Christ than you can truly trust in Christ without turning away from sin." -**Charles Spurgeon**

We have already established that Jesus' arrival marked the fulfillment of God's promised Kingdom, as foretold by the prophets, and that His coming brought the presence of the Holy Spirit among us. Through His ministry, death, and resurrection, Israel experienced a remarkable resurrection and renewal as a nation, leading to the establishment of the Kingdom of God within this renewed Israel.

Before ascending to the heavenly presence of the Father, Jesus entrusted His apostles with the commission to preach the Good News of the Kingdom, and share the keys necessary for entering this Kingdom. Therefore, our study will center around the significance of entering the Kingdom of God, examining three crucial passages that illuminate the appropriate responses to preaching the Good News.

Firstly, let us consider the preaching of Jesus Himself, as recorded in Mark 1:14-15: *"Now after John was arrested, Jesus came to Galilee proclaiming the good news of God and saying, 'The time is fulfilled, and the kingdom of God has come near; repent, and believe in the good news.'"*

In these verses, Jesus proclaimed the Good News of the Kingdom and presented the appropriate response to His message—repentance and belief. While some may argue that this passage was specifically addressed to a Jewish audience, a comprehensive study of the New Testament reveals that these two responses—repentance and belief—are foundational and applicable to all who receive the Kingdom message.

Secondly, it was not only Jesus but also the Apostle Paul who emphasized these responses, extending their significance to a broader audience of Jews and Gentiles. Acts 20:20-21 provides further insight: *"I did not shrink from doing anything helpful, proclaiming the message to you and teaching you publicly and from house to house, as I testified to both Jews and Greeks about repentance toward God and faith toward our Lord Jesus."* Here, Paul highlights the importance of both repentance toward God and faith in the Lord Jesus Christ, emphasizing that these responses are relevant not only for the Jews but also for the Gentiles.

Even in the era of the second-generation disciples, the book of Hebrews exhorted its readers in Hebrews 6:1: "Therefore, let us go on toward perfection, leaving behind the basic teaching about Christ and not laying the foundation again: repentance from dead works and faith toward God."

The combined message from Jesus, Paul, and the writer of Hebrews underscores the profound significance of these two spiritual responses: repentance and faith.

But why is repentance toward God crucial? The Hebrew term *"teshuvah,"* meaning *"to turn and return,"* was rooted in the historical context of exile and served as a call for Israel to forsake their idolatry and sins, returning to the Lord Yahweh, the one true God. Similarly, through repentance, we are called to turn away from our sins and realign ourselves with the Father in His Kingdom, experiencing His love and grace as we did before being separated from Him.

Belief, the second response, carries its own weight. In Hebrew, *"emunah"* conveys the concepts of *"steadfastness* and *faithfulness,"* and it refers to the object of belief, which is God Himself—steadfast, faithful, and true to His covenant. In Greek, *"pistis"* encompasses the ideas of "faith, trust, and dependability." Therefore, we are invited to place our trust in the Gospel of God's Kingdom and in Jesus, the anointed King of this kingdom. The essence of this confidence and dependence is what we describe as allegiance or faithful surrender to the King's power and authority.

Consequently, the Gospel's plea to us today remains unchanged: repent and believe. This plea calls us to return to the Lord as our only true and real God, repenting of our sins and surrendering to His Kingdom through our allegiance and loyalty to the Anointed King, Jesus Christ. In doing so, we embrace the transformative power of the Kingdom, experiencing its blessings, peace, and eternal life.

Prayer:

Blessed are You Lord God, King of the Universe, for providing for us the way to return to Your Kingdom by repentance and faith-allegiance to your Anointed King, Your Son, Jesus Christ.

CONFESSION AND BAPTISM:

Verbal & Dramatic Expressions of Faith

27 As many of you as were baptized into Christ have clothed yourselves with Christ. - **Galatians 3:26–27**

We explored in the last chapter the crucial spiritual responses of repentance and faith. These paths are vital for every individual to embark upon. Repentance involves turning away from our sins, while faith entails approaching God and placing our trust in Him. Now, let us delve deeper into how we can demonstrate our faith in two significant ways.

Faith, understood as trust, loyalty, and allegiance to the Lord and King, requires public demonstration. Just as in the Middle Ages, when a squire would become a knight through a dubbing ceremony, where he knelt before a knight, lord, or king who tapped him on the shoulder with a sword to signify his new position and obligation, faith also necessitates public declarations. Think of wedding rings, vows, and a kiss that symbolize love and publicly established relationships. Similarly, faith, as a means of establishing and maintaining a relationship with God, must be communicated, and demonstrated in a visible manner.

The first public expression of faith is confession. The apostle Paul highlights its importance in Romans 10:9-10. Paul emphasizes that we must confess with our mouths that Jesus is Lord and believe in our hearts that God raised Him from the dead. Confession allows us to publicly declare our faith in Jesus, recognizing Him as our Lord and King. We see this example in Acts 8, when Philip the Evangelist encounters the Ethiopian eunuch who desires baptism. Philip tells him, "If you believe with all your heart, you may." The eunuch responds by confessing that Jesus Christ is the Son of God. Confession plays a significant role in publicly proclaiming our trust in God and acknowledging His reign as King and Lord through Jesus Christ.

The second expression of faith is baptism. The term "baptism" originates from the Greek word "baptidzo," meaning to dip, immerse, or submerge.

Baptism carries symbolic meaning, as the Jews practiced it as a ritual purification before entering the temple. John the Baptist baptized Jesus, and during His baptism, the Holy Spirit descended, and the voice of God confirmed Jesus' identity as the Son of God. Before ascending to heaven, Jesus commanded His disciples to make disciples of all nations, with baptism being an essential component of that process. Baptism is a powerful act of faith that represents our identification with Jesus in His death, burial, and resurrection. It signifies the death of our old selves, the cleansing of sin, and the acquisition of new life in Christ Jesus (Matthew 3; Romans 6:1-6; 2 Corinthians 5:17–19).

In summary, faith requires both public proclamation and demonstration. We publicly affirm our faith in Jesus as Lord and display our loyalty to Him through confession. Baptism serves as a profound symbolic ritual, representing our union with Christ's death, burial, and resurrection. It signifies our new life in Him and our commitment to live as His disciples. Our faith demands public expression, just as a couple displays their love through wedding vows and kisses. Let us boldly confess Jesus and be baptized, demonstrating our confidence, commitment, and allegiance to Jesus, our Lord, and King.

Prayer:

Blessed are You, O Lord, King of the Universe, that You have given us confession and baptism to express and demonstrate our faith in You, through your Son that You have as Lord and King of all Creation, Amen!

ON BAPTISM:

His Story & Our Salvation

"Baptism incorporates us into Christ and forms us into God's people. This sacrament forgives sins, grants new birth, and imparts the Holy Spirit."   -**Thomas Aquinas**

There was a wise and gentle preacher began his preaching, *"Today, my friends, we embark on a journey to unveil the true essence of water baptism. It is not merely a ritual but a powerful demonstration of our faith in Jesus Christ as our Lord and King. Let us dive deep into the river of truth and discover the beauty of this sacred sacrament."*

He started shouting, "Listen, all of you! Let us remember that God reigns in this world through His Anointed Son, Jesus Christ. He appointed Jesus to be the Lord and King in His Kingdom. Through His death, burial, and resurrection, Jesus demonstrated His identity as the Messiah, the Christ, the Savior King. We are now called to repent and believe in this Good News of God's Kingdom, surrendering ourselves to His reign by confessing Jesus as Lord and accepting His Kingship through baptism."

Baptism is not a means to earn salvation through our own works. Unlike the Jewish practice of self-immersion known as "Mikvah", Christian baptism is an act performed by one person upon another. It signifies the baptismal immersion of the subject by the one who baptizes, representing a profound act of submission and surrender."

Drawing their attention to the Scriptures, the preacher quoted John 6:29, where Jesus declared, *"The work of God is this: to believe in the one He has sent."* He continued, *"Through baptism, we publicly declare our faith in Jesus and acknowledge that our salvation rests solely on His finished work on the cross (Acts 2:36). It is a profound act of surrender to Jesus, recognizing that even repentance—the ability to turn away from sin and turn to God—is a gift bestowed upon us by the Holy Spirit, as Acts 5:31-32 reveals."*

As the sun's golden rays danced through the branches, casting a warm glow upon the eager listeners, the teacher went on to share another layer of meaning. *"Baptism is a symbolic representation of the new covenant between God and His people,"* he explained. *"In the Old Testament, circumcision served as a physical sign of the covenant given to Israel. But in the New Testament, baptism becomes the circumcision of the heart—a spiritual transformation brought about by the sacrificial death of Jesus on the cross (Colossians 2:11-13)."*

With enthusiasm in his voice, the preacher quoted Romans 6:4, *"We were therefore buried with Him through baptism into death in order that, just as Christ was raised from the dead through the glory of the Father, we too may live a new life."* He continued, *"Through baptism, we identify ourselves with Jesus' death, burial, and resurrection. It is a powerful symbol of our union with God the Father, Jesus, and the Holy Spirit (Romans 6:1-6; 2 Corinthians 5:17–20)."*

The villagers listened attentively, their hearts stirred by the preacher's words. He then spoke of the profound purpose that baptism holds for believers. *"Baptism is not a mere act to secure a place in heaven after death,"* he emphasized. *"It marks our first step on the path of discipleship—a commission to go forth and make disciples of all nations, spreading the image and likeness of God throughout the world."*

Quoting Matthew 28:19, the teacher reminded them of the word of the Lord Jesus, *"Go and make disciples of all nations, baptizing them in the name of the Father and of the Son and of the Holy Spirit."* He added, *"Baptism aligns us with God's mission through Jesus and empowers us with the Holy Spirit to fulfill this purpose (Romans 8:9-14; 2 Corinthians 3:17-18). It is an exciting beginning of our Christian journey of total transformation as we follow the leading of the Holy Spirit, imitating and living like Jesus."*

As the lesson ended, the preacher's voice grew tender yet resolute. *"Water baptism holds a deep spiritual significance in the life of every believer,"* he proclaimed. *"It is a public demonstration of our faith in Jesus Christ as our Lord and King. Through baptism, we acknowledge our union with God, participation in the new covenant, and commitment to discipleship and mission. Baptism is potent representation of our faith to the one who saves us—and a step toward carrying out the task that our Savior have entrusted to us."*

With eyes filled with anticipation and hearts ablaze with newfound understanding, the preacher boldly shouted, *"What are you waiting for? Decide for yourself, repent, and call upon the Lord for forgiveness of your sin by faith demonstrated through the waters of baptism"* (cf. Acts 22:16). The villagers embraced the call to be baptized and embark on the thrilling path of following Jesus, ready to make a positive impact on the world through their faith and obedience.

Thus, the story of God's Kingdom continues to be passionately retold, calling for a demonstration of faith and allegiance to the King through baptism from one generation to the next, weaving its way into the tapestry of believers' lives. Baptism remains a testament to their faith, a symbol of their union with Christ, and a catalyst for their transformative journey of discipleship. May you, too, embrace this sacred practice and embark on the thrilling adventure of following Jesus, leaving an indelible mark upon the world through the power of your unwavering faith express through repentance and baptism.

Prayer:

Blessed are You, O Lord, King of the universe. We offer our heartfelt gratitude for the message of the good news of Your kingdom and the profound gift of water baptism. Through this sacred act, we enter Your presence, united with You through Your Son, Jesus Christ, and by the power of the Holy Spirit. Amen.

PART THREE

After responding to the Call of discipleship, what next? Explore what it means to be a disciple and fulfill your calling to preach the Gospel of the Kingdom.

Discover the value of the church as a place where disciples can grow in their love for God, one another, and the community. Learn what it means to be a follower of Jesus Christ and how you can contribute to the church's mission of transforming the world.

Get ready to accept your role as a disciple of the Kingdom fully and be a part in fulfilling the Jesus' Commission given to disciples.

ON BEING A DISCIPLE:

Called for A Mission

"A disciple is not someone who merely affirms a certain set of beliefs, but someone who loves and follows Jesus in every aspect of life." - **Dietrich Bonhoeffer.**

In the previous chapter, we uncovered the profound truth about water baptism and its connection to the call to discipleship. Now, let us embark on a deeper exploration of what it truly means to be a disciple, the essence of discipleship, and our mission as followers of Christ Jesus. These concepts are intricately intertwined and hold immense significance in shaping our lives as Christians. Join me on this enlightening journey as we uncover the essence of discipleship.

At its very core, a disciple is a devoted follower and learner of a specific teacher or master. In the realm of

Christianity, being a disciple means wholeheartedly following Jesus Christ as our Lord and King. Discipleship goes far beyond a mere acceptance of Jesus; it involves a complete commitment to understanding and embodying His teachings, walking in His footsteps, and imitating His way of life. In fact, the early followers of Jesus were initially referred to as disciples before the term "Christians" came into existence (Acts 11:26). As disciples, we enjoy a close relationship with our Master, Jesus, who molds us into His likeness with the assistance of more experienced disciples. These fellow disciples play a vital role in our growth and maturity, teaching, rebuking, correcting, and training us in righteousness through prayers and through the Holy Scriptures (Ephesians 3:14-21; Timothy 3:16-17). This transformative process is known as discipleship.

Discipleship is not a one-time event but an ongoing spiritual growth and transformation journey. It entails aligning our lives with the image of Christ, allowing our thoughts, attitudes, and actions to reflect His love and holiness. This commitment accompanies us throughout our entire lives as we continuously learn, develop, and mature in our faith. We are not called to be mere believers or passive church members; rather, we are called to be faithful disciples of the Lord Jesus, commissioned to make disciples of all nations (Matthew 28:18-20).

There are three fundamental characteristics that distinguish true disciples. Firstly, they abide in the words of Jesus (John 8:31). While our faith revolves around Jesus Himself, our understanding of Him deepens as we delve into the Holy Scriptures (John 5:39–40). The Scriptures not only teach us to place our faith in Jesus for salvation but also equip us to carry out good works for the glory of the Lord (2 Timothy 3:15–17).

Secondly, true disciples abide in God's love. Our love for God and others serves as a tangible display of our discipleship. The love we possess for God and our acts of kindness and service towards others exemplify us as disciples of Jesus. Jesus Himself emphasized the paramount importance of love, stating that it serves as the defining characteristic of His disciples (John 13:34–35). Love heals the damage that sin has done to our relationship with God and promotes peace among people. Through love, we experience union with God and eternal life in the present moment   (1 John 5:13).

Lastly, true disciples bear abundant fruit for the glory of God. As disciples, we are called to bear fruit reflecting the Holy Spirit's transformative work in our lives. Galatians 5:22–23 describes this fruit as *"love, joy, peace, forbearance, kindness, goodness, faithfulness, gentleness, and self-control."* These fruits equip us to bring about a bountiful harvest as people are drawn to the Kingdom of God by the fragrance of our lives, which mirrors the love and life of our Master Teacher, Jesus (Romans 1:13; 2 Corinthians 2:15–16).

In conclusion, being a disciple of Jesus entails abiding in His words, abiding in His love, and bearing abundant fruit through the power of the Holy Spirit. It is an ongoing journey of learning, growing, and imitating our Master. As disciples, we are called to embark on the most adventurous and fulfilling path of following Jesus.

One of the most crucial pieces of advice I can offer is to earnestly seek the guidance of a trusted minister, pastor, or seasoned disciple who possesses wisdom and experience in the faith. . Surrender yourself to their mentorship, allowing them to nurture and lead you on your journey of spiritual growth and maturity in the Lord for you to be prepared and equipped to fulfill the mission to make disciples for the Lord. May you embrace the essence of discipleship and discover the joy and purpose it brings to your life.

Prayer:

Blessed are You O Lord, King of the Universe. We are grateful for your calling and for inviting us to become disciples of your Son, Jesus. Please grant us the strength to follow His teachings and remain faithful and steadfast in His Love. May His Holy Spirit guide us and help us to bear abundant fruits in our lives, drawing many people closer to You and Your Kingdom.

THE CHURCH:

The Community of Disciples

"The church is called to be the visible community of God's love, reconciling the world to himself." - **Desmond Tutu.**

When people embrace the Gospel of the Kingdom and surrender their life to Jesus as Lord and King, they become disciples and find their place within the church community (Acts 2:41). The term "church" comes from the Greek word "ekklesia," which signifies a summoned assembly of people. The church is a gathering of individuals called together to worship and serve God. Just as the Kingdom of God represents His authority and reign, the church is the community of citizens under the rule of the King. In this chapter, we will explore the vital role of the church in the lives of Jesus' followers.

It is crucial to remember that the church emerges because of the proclamation of the Gospel. The Gospel carries the message of the Kingdom, and the church comprises those who have responded to this proclamation. However, we must also understand that the church is not the Message itself nor the Savior. Rather, it serves as the bearer of the Saving Message, the Kingdom's Gospel. Church members are former sinners who have received salvation solely by God's grace through Jesus, the anointed Lord and King (Acts 4:12).

So, if the church is not the Message nor the Savior, what role does it play in the life of a Christian? It is a nurturing community. The church functions as a family, nurturing disciples and encouraging its members to a life of devotion. Acts 2:42 reveals that when the church was established, people devoted themselves to *"the apostles' teaching and fellowship, to the breaking of bread, and prayer."*

Devotion to the apostles' teaching involves embracing and studying Jesus' words and doctrines. Today, these teachings have been recorded in the Holy Scriptures. When we commit ourselves to reading and studying the Scriptures with genuine devotion, they teach, inspire, and offer us hope (Romans 15:4).

Devotion to fellowship calls for a life of sharing and active participation. The early believers regularly gathered and assembled, sharing God's blessings, spreading the Good News, and caring for those in need. Being present and engaged in these gatherings is crucial for the growth of all Christians, and our active involvement in the church reflects our spiritual well-being (Hebrews 10:23–26).

The act of breaking bread in the disciples' meetings signifies their unity and familial bond. It harks back to Jesus and the apostles during the Passover Meal when they instituted what we commonly refer to as the Lord's Supper. This fellowship meal symbolizes their gratitude, or Eucharist, for being the New Israel of God in the New Exodus, with Jesus as the New Moses leading them from the Dominion of Darkness into the Kingdom of Light (1 Corinthians 11:23–26; Colossians 1:11–14).

Lastly, commitment to prayer is of utmost importance. Prayer is the lifeblood of our faith. Devoting ourselves to prayer provides constant access to God's presence. It is the means through which we communicate with God, surrender to His will, and receive empowerment from the Holy Spirit as we immerse ourselves in His presence through this spiritual practice.

In summary, the church consists of disciples who have responded to the Gospel message. It is crucial to nurture and guide these followers on their spiritual journey by involving them in teaching, fellowship, shared meals, and in prayers. As disciples walk the path of discipleship, the church provides an environment for them to develop, grow, and mature in faith. Let us recognize the power of the church to unite, equip, and guide us as we follow Jesus and manifest the Kingdom of God here on earth

Prayer:

Blessed are You, Lord, King of the Universe. We thank You for the gift of the church as the disciples' community. Help us, Lord, to recognize the importance of the church in our lives and to be able to fully participate in its teachings, fellowship, communion, and prayer. As we try to live out our discipleship and promote the Gospel of the Kingdom, may the church be a source of strength, unity, and growth. In Christ Jesus. Amen.

OUR OFFERING

Disciples' Daily Lives

"Being a disciple means living out our faith in the ordinary moments of everyday life, turning the mundane into the sacred." - **Richard J. Foster**

The life of a disciple is intricately connected to the life of the church, where they reside and labor as a united group, sharing in the Kingdom of the Lord. In our previous chapter, we explored the collective devotions of the church, driven by a common objective, purpose, and mission. Now, let us delve into their daily lives and discover what a believer does daily and what influences their existence.

In his letter to the Romans (12:1), the apostle Paul addresses us as followers of Jesus, urging us, "in view of God's mercy, to offer your bodies as a living sacrifice, holy and pleasing to God—this is your true and proper worship." The language used here carries echoes of liturgical practices in the temple.

However, there is a fundamental difference now. Unlike the previous sacrificial system involving animals, disciples are called to present themselves as living sacrifices. They are to offer their whole beings, not lifeless animals, as pure and acceptable sacrifices to God. To be holy means to be cleansed and set apart from anything that defiles or contaminates. To be acceptable means that God has authorized us. Just as the high priest would inspect the animal sacrifices, our Lord examines our devotion. Consequently, our worship of God is not confined to gatherings or weekly assemblies but extends to every day of our lives.

Our lives, each day anew,

An offering to God, so true.

In how we spend our time and care,

Our worship shines with love, service, and pray'r."

Psalm 1:2 tells us, "But their delight is in the law of the Lord, and on his law, they meditate day and night." Each day presents an opportunity for us to delight in the Lord's law, and feast upon it. It is a time for meditation, focusing our minds and hearts on the Scriptures until their truth permeates our being. Meditation is a focused prayer that aligns your thoughts with the mind of the Lord revealed through the sacred scriptures. Prayerful meditation, akin to chewing food, is the disciple's way of savoring God's words, allowing them to penetrate and nourish their minds, aligning them with the Mind of the Lord.

During the early days of Christianity, every day was an occasion for disciples to gather for worship in designated places and in the homes of fellow believers. It was also a chance for them to share the Good News that Jesus is the Messiah, the chosen Christ and King who brings salvation to many. Acts 5:42 tells us, *"And every day, in the temple and from house to house, they did not cease teaching and preaching Jesus as the Christ."*

Furthermore, our daily existence should not be self-centered but focused on serving our fellow disciples and others. The writer of Hebrews encourages us to exhort and support one another daily. Exhortation and encouragement were vital even in the early days of the church. Through these actions, our fellow disciples become the antidote to the hardening and deceitfulness of sin.

> *Hebrews 3:13 states, "But encourage one another daily, as long as it is called 'Today,' so that sin's deceitfulness may harden none of you."*

Worship, meditation on God's Word, gathering for fellowship and proclamation, and serving one another are all integral aspects of discipleship. Each day presents a fresh opportunity to live out our faith, to deepen our love and commitment to the Lord, and to impact the lives of those around us. Let us cherish the beauty and significance of our daily journey as disciples of Jesus.

Prayer:

Blessed are You, O Lord, King of the Universe. We give thanks to You, Father, for the daily blessings of worship and service. Fill us with Your Holy Spirit as we meditate on Your words, proclaim the Good News, and gather with our fellow believers to exhort and encourage one another. In the name of Christ Jesus, we pray. Amen.

NEW HEAVENS AND NEW EARTH:

The Hope of Disciples

"The language of the new heaven and new earth… is the language of hope for a transformed world in which God's justice will be established and all creation will flourish."

-Marcus Borg

Disciples lead rich, purposeful, and far-reaching lives beyond their weekly gatherings. Their passionate prayers, personal devotion to God's Word, and collective worship shape the very fabric of their daily existence. Throughout the annals of history, disciples have left an indelible mark on societies and civilizations, yet the world still grapples with the enduring presence of sin and darkness. In the face of these challenges, disciples eagerly anticipate the ultimate resolution—a time when every thought and action will align perfectly with God's will. This chapter takes us on a journey of hope, exploring the profound vision of a new heaven and earth—a hope deeply embedded in the Hebrew scriptures and reverberating throughout the New Testament.

Within the pages of Hebrew literature, the book of Isaiah shines with promises of new heavens and a new earth. In Isaiah 65:17, we read, "Behold, I will build a new earth and a new set of heavens. The previous events won't be recalled or even thought of." These prophecies were written during the trying times of the Babylonian captivity, offering solace and hope to those enduring the depths of despair. They served as a reminder that the Lord had pledged a complete and radical transformation akin to the birth of new heavens and a new earth.

The concept of new heavens and new earth also finds its place in the New Testament, as eloquently expressed in 2 Peter 3:13: *"But in keeping with his promise, we are looking forward to a new heaven and a new earth, where righteousness dwells."* The apostle Peter urged the early Christians to cling tenaciously to God's promises, including the expectation of a future characterized by new heavens and a new earth, in the face of widespread immorality, injustice, and unbelief.

In the book of Revelation, an apocalyptic masterpiece, hope springs forth for a persecuted and suffering church. Revelation 21:1 unveils a vision: *"Then I saw 'a new heaven and a new earth,' for the first heaven and the first earth had passed away, and there was no longer any sea."* Additionally, Revelation 21:4 reassures us that God will tenderly wipe away every tear from our eyes, eradicating death, mourning, crying, and pain. The old order of things will be no more.

Nevertheless, the exact timing of these events remains veiled in mystery. Just as the precise moment of the Lord's Second Coming eludes us, the end of the old world to make way for the new heavens and new earth will arrive unexpectedly, like a thief in the night (2 Peter 3:9). The perspective of the Apostle Paul further emphasizes that the entire world eagerly anticipates the fulfillment of this promise. Romans 8:21 proclaims that the entire creation will be set free from its bondage to decay and will partake in the glorious freedom of being children of God. The groaning of creation echoes the deep yearning within the hearts of disciples for their adoption and the redemption of their bodies (Romans 8:22–23).

Interestingly, Paul also teaches that the advent of the new heavens and earth has already begun through the acceptance of Jesus as Lord and King. When an individual accepts Christ Jesus, they undergo a transformation, becoming a new creation and signaling the dawn of the promise of new heavens and a new earth. This transformation occurs as they surrender to the message of the Gospel of the Kingdom and pledge their unwavering allegiance to the Anointed King. As 2 Corinthians 5:17 joyfully proclaims, *"So if anyone is in Christ, there is a new creation: everything old has passed away; look, new things have come into being!"*

Herein lies the remarkable news—the very essence of the Kingdom's Gospel. By accepting Jesus as your Lord and Christ and surrendering your life to His reign, you can become a part of this new creation. Through repentance and baptism, you bear witness to your faith and loyalty to Him. In this beautiful act, you receive forgiveness and the promised Holy Spirit, and you are sealed as a cherished member of God's Kingdom—a new creation, prepared for the New Heavens and a New Earth (Acts 2:36–38; 2 Corinthians 5:17; Revelation 21:1-4).

Prayer:

Blessed are You, O Lord, King of the Universe! We offer our gratitude, Father, for Your promise of the New Heavens and New Earth. We exalt You for graciously inviting and calling us to be active participants in this glorious New Creation. We pray in the name of Your Son, Jesus, our Lord and King. Amen!

CONCLUSION

We started reading this book with a fascinating tale about the renowned composer Giacomo Puccini, whose devoted friends finished his unfinished masterpiece. Their dedication to preserving Puccini's legacy led them to fill in the missing notes and melodies, ensuring that his music would continue to resonate with audiences and evoke profound emotions. Similarly, our Lord and King, Jesus, initiated a magnificent spiritual symphony, proclaiming the Good News of God's Kingdom and demonstrating its power through his teachings, miraculous healings, and selfless service to the community.

However, as the final crescendo of Jesus' earthly ministry approached, he knew he would soon depart. He entrusted his disciples with the task of continuing the work of salvation, healing, and bringing hope to those in need. With his crucifixion, burial, and triumphant resurrection, a new chapter was written in the symphony of God's redemptive plan. The baton was passed to his followers, and it was their turn to carry forward the melody of love, grace, and transformation.

My journey as a disciple of Jesus began at the tender age of 17 when I first encountered the life-changing power of the Gospel. In 1991, I decided to repent and be baptized, eagerly embracing the call to follow Jesus Christ. Overflowing with enthusiasm and a burning desire to learn more about Jesus and his teachings, I eagerly awaited each Sunday, immersing myself in the fellowship of believers, raising my voice in heartfelt hymns of worship, and eagerly listening to Bible studies and sermons that deepened my understanding of the Savior and the church.

Those early years were filled with an insatiable hunger for knowledge and spiritual growth. Yet, as I delved deeper into the teachings of Jesus, I began to realize that discipleship was not merely a passive endeavor of accumulating information or attending religious services. It required actively embodying the love and kindness exemplified by our Lord. I understood that I needed to go beyond being a recipient of spiritual nourishment and become an instrument of God's grace and mercy in the lives of others.

This profound realization led me to embrace the role of a servant in the church. I recognized that it was not enough to be content with consuming spiritual insights; I needed to actively contribute to the growth and well-being of the community of believers. With this conviction, I embarked on a rigorous course of study, equipping myself to serve as a youth minister in our church. The journey was not without its challenges, but the joy of sharing the transformative message of the Gospel with young hearts made every step worthwhile.

As the years unfolded and I embraced my role as a minister of the Tuao Church of Christ, I discovered that my journey as a disciple extended far beyond the boundaries of my specific ministry. It became clear to me that I was responsible for proclaiming the Gospel and making disciples who, in turn, could make disciples themselves. However, fulfilling this mission required more than just a surface-level understanding of the Gospel. It demanded a deep mastery of and familiarity with its content.

In the pages of this book, we see that the Gospel is not a mere collection of Bible lessons we share for the sake of salvation. It is not a set of rigid laws to be obeyed, nor is it a series of sequential steps to follow. It is not about proving the superiority or correctness of our church over others. Rather, as revealed in the sacred scriptures, the Gospel is the proclamation that the Kingdom of God has arrived through the Lordship and Kingship of Jesus, anointed with the

Spirit of the Lord.

"The Kingdom's Gospel," the book you hold in your hands, represents a continuation of the work that Jesus initiated during his earthly ministry. It serves as a guide, showing us the important notes, we should play, the wonderful melodies that listeners should hear, and the magnificent harmony from which we invite others to join in.

My heartfelt desire is that you will be inspired and moved as you delve into these pages. I hope to persuade you, dear reader, to consider the transformative power of the Kingdom's Gospel in your own life. May its message resonate deep within you, stirring a desire to invite others to walk the path of discipleship, follow in Jesus's footsteps, and become bearers of the message of hope, love, and redemption found in the Gospel of the Kingdom. Together, let us create a symphony of faith reverberating worldwide.

AFTERWORD

PLEDGING OUR ALLEGIANCE:

Following Jesus as Lord and King

To all readers who, like the early listeners of the Gospel, ponder the timeless question, "What must I do to be saved?" – let us respond with the essence of this book.

Firstly, listen to the message of The Kingdom's Gospel, proclaiming the Good News that has resonated from the dawn of creation to this very moment: God is the King! He reigns supreme over all, eternally sovereign. His dominion stretches from Eden to Israel, the chosen nation, and to every corner of the globe, culminating in these Last Days through His Son, Jesus Christ – crucified for our sins, buried, and resurrected as the anointed Lord and King. (Mark 1:14-15; Luke 4:43; 1 Corinthians 15:1-5)

Secondly, Repent or Turn to the Lord by turning away from your sins. Repentance calls us to return to Yahweh as the King of our lives. Like the Prodigal Son who turned back to his Father, you too are invited to forsake your sins and return to God the Father. (Luke 15:11-32; 24:45-47)

Thirdly, Believe in the Good News. Saving belief means trusting in the message of the Kingdom of God by surrendering your life to Jesus as your Lord and King. Belief entails a faithful allegiance, submitting to the Lordship of the Messiah who died, was buried, and rose again – anointed by the Father to reign eternally over His Kingdom. (Acts 2:36; 17:7; Corinthians 15:1-5,24-28)

Fourthly, Confess. Verbally acknowledge that Jesus is the Lord of your life. This declaration of allegiance must be made publicly. Proclaiming your submission to the Lordship of King Jesus is crucial. (Romans 10:9-10)

Fifthly, Water Baptism. Those who trust in and publicly confess Jesus as Lord and King must demonstrate their faith through water baptism, symbolizing their union in the death, burial, and resurrection of Jesus. (Romans 6:3-5; Acts 2:38)

Sixthly, Live as a New Creation, embracing a new way of life in fellowship with God through King

Jesus, empowered by the Holy Spirit. Worship and serve God alongside fellow disciples of the King, the church of the Lord, embodying the Kingdom of God. (Acts 2:41-47; 2 Corinthians 5:17)

Seventh, Joyfully live a life of love. The God of this Kingdom is the God of Love. His chosen King sacrificially gave His life for our salvation. As King, He commanded us to love God and love our neighbors. Living out this command is the visible proof that we are His Kingdom Disciples, already passed from death to Life Eternal. (Matthew 22:36-40; Mark 12:28-31; 1 John 3:14-15, 4:7-12)

Eighth, Faithfully fulfill the Commission given by the Lord and King. In this Kingdom, we worship not merely as forgiven people but as empowered agents of the Holy Spirit, commissioned to make disciples of all nations, extending His dominion worldwide by spreading God's love incarnate in Christ Jesus – now embodied by His disciples, the bearers of His Kingdom. (Matthew 28:18-20; Mark 16:15-16)

The choice is yours, but time is fleeting. Seize this opportunity to follow Jesus, the Lord and King, before it's too late! Embrace The Kingdom's Gospel, repent, believe, confess, be baptized, live as a new creation, joyfully live a life of love, and faithfully carry out the King's commission. Don't let this chance for salvation slip away. (Acts 22:16; 2 Corinthians 6:1-2)

Come, let us follow Jesus, the Lord and King. Today!

ACKNOWLEDGEMENT

This book represents the fulfillment of a lifelong dream. For as long as I can remember, I have harbored a deep aspiration to write a book centered around the Bible, with a particular focus on the profound topic of the Gospel.

Before my discovery of the profound works of scholars such as N.T. Wright, Scot McKnight, and Matthew W. Bates, my passion for delving into the depths of the Gospel and presenting it within its biblical framework for the common reader had already taken root. The knowledge and insights gained from their insightful books have further fueled my desire to explore this timeless subject.

I am deeply grateful to the mentors who have played a significant role in my journey with the Bible. First and foremost, I would like to express my appreciation to **Wilbert Tupas,** my co-minister at **Tondo Church of Christ**. He has been a constant source of encouragement even he is now in U.S.

always pushing me to delve deeper into the scholarly works and uncover hidden insights.

I am also indebted to bro. *John Mark Hicks,* whose generosity in sharing his books has broadened my understanding of narrative theology and the overarching storyline of the Bible. His teachings have provided me with a fresh perspective and deepened my appreciation for the rich tapestry of God's Word.

Lastly, I would like to acknowledge the members of the "***Online Biblical Books:*** A Review and Discussion Group" on Facebook. Your presence and engagement have been a constant source of inspiration and encouragement. Your shared passion for learning and exploring the depths of the sacred scriptures have spurred me on to continue my own quest for knowledge.

Thank you for joining me on this exploration of the Kingdom's Gospel and its profound message. May this book inspire and enlighten us as we journey deeper into the Kingdom's Gospel. With the guidance of these friends and mentors, with the advancements of modern technology, it has become easier to embark on a writing journey such as this.

ABOUT THE AUTHOR

Jhun Ma

I am Eduardo Ma Jr., known affectionately as bro. Jhun Ma among my friends and brethren. I am happily married to my lovely wife, Babes Ma, and together we have been blessed with three remarkable children: Jed, who is 13 years old, Jacob, who is 11 years old, and John, who is 7 years old. Currently, I serve as a minister at the Tuao Church of Christ in Tuao East, Cagayan Valley. Our church is dedicated to serving the communities of Barangay Taribubu and other neighboring barangays, where our cherished members reside.

Alongside my ministry, I also fulfill the role of a Secondary School Teacher at Tuao Vocational and Technical School's main campus. There, I have the privilege of teaching English to eager young minds. Throughout my life, I have nurtured a deep-seated aspiration to become an author. Balancing the responsibilities of church and school, finding time for introspection and writing has been a challenge. Nevertheless, I am grateful for the blessings of modern technology, which have equipped me with the tools and afforded me the time to embark on the writing journey I have longed to pursue. Every word penned is dedicated to bringing glory to the Father, and I am humbled by this opportunity to share my thoughts and experiences through the pages of my books.

https://www.facebook.com/jhunma2000

PRAISE FOR AUTHOR

"The book is superb! It gives a refreshing take on the Gospel, gives insight about the Good News of the Messiah in ways not popular in some Christian circles, moves the reader to practice the theology behind the Biblical narrative. Indeed, the disciple must follow the King, Jesus the Messiah!" - ANGEL GIDEON RODRIGUEZ, Applications Specialist at Scientific Biotech Specialties Inc.,

"Excellent effort by the author to write this book. It is a concise overview of the Bible, walking the reader through how the gospel message came about, its impact on humanity, and the importance of the disciples continuing the work that Jesus has started. The author also encourages the readers to do more than just "being a recipient of spiritual nourishment"; and that is to "become an instrument of God's grace and mercy in the lives of others." - PETER LIM, Elder, Pasir Panjang Church of Christ, Singapore

"The book's contents present a very focused account of

the New Testament's message about Jesus Christ that is given to the world. Ma succeeds in staying very close to the sacred text itself and engages the reader in meaningful ways. As a lifelong Bible student, I was impressed with the clarity and practicality of Ma's rendition of the good news about Jesus, even after over 50 years of reading similar presentations. I find it easy to recommend this book." -   DONALD PRANTL, Retired Teacher, Former Resident of Texas, North Carolina, Arkansas, and Honduras,

"The Kingdom Gospel"! It is well written and provides the reader a concise factual summary of what the Kingdom of God is all about. It is not too long or too short, just right!! In fact, I plan to print this and give it to one of my ex-convict friends who is still struggling with understanding the gospel. I believe that this devotional book is just what he needs."- ED POBLETE, Retired Missionary and Outreach Minister, Ada, Oklahoma

"Jhun Ma's book is a good resource for teaching seekers and new believers about basic Christianity."- K. REX BUTTS, Author and Lead Minister/Pastor at Newark Church Of Christ.

"The Kingdom's Gospel" by Bro. Jhun Ma is a remarkable piece of literature that blends simplicity with depth, making it an ideal companion for both seasoned believers and newcomers to the faith. This book stands out for its straightforwardness, presenting complex

theological concepts in a manner that is accessible and applicable to daily life. Make sure that you tell your congregation to get a copy each. I'm sure that this book will encourage them to be part of the Kingdom ministry.
" - AL ECHEGOYEN, Minister, Cabatuan Church of Christ (Iloilo, Philippines)

Made in the USA
Middletown, DE
30 May 2024